CICERO

Leaders of the Ancient World

CICERO

Zoe Lowery and

Fiona Forsyth

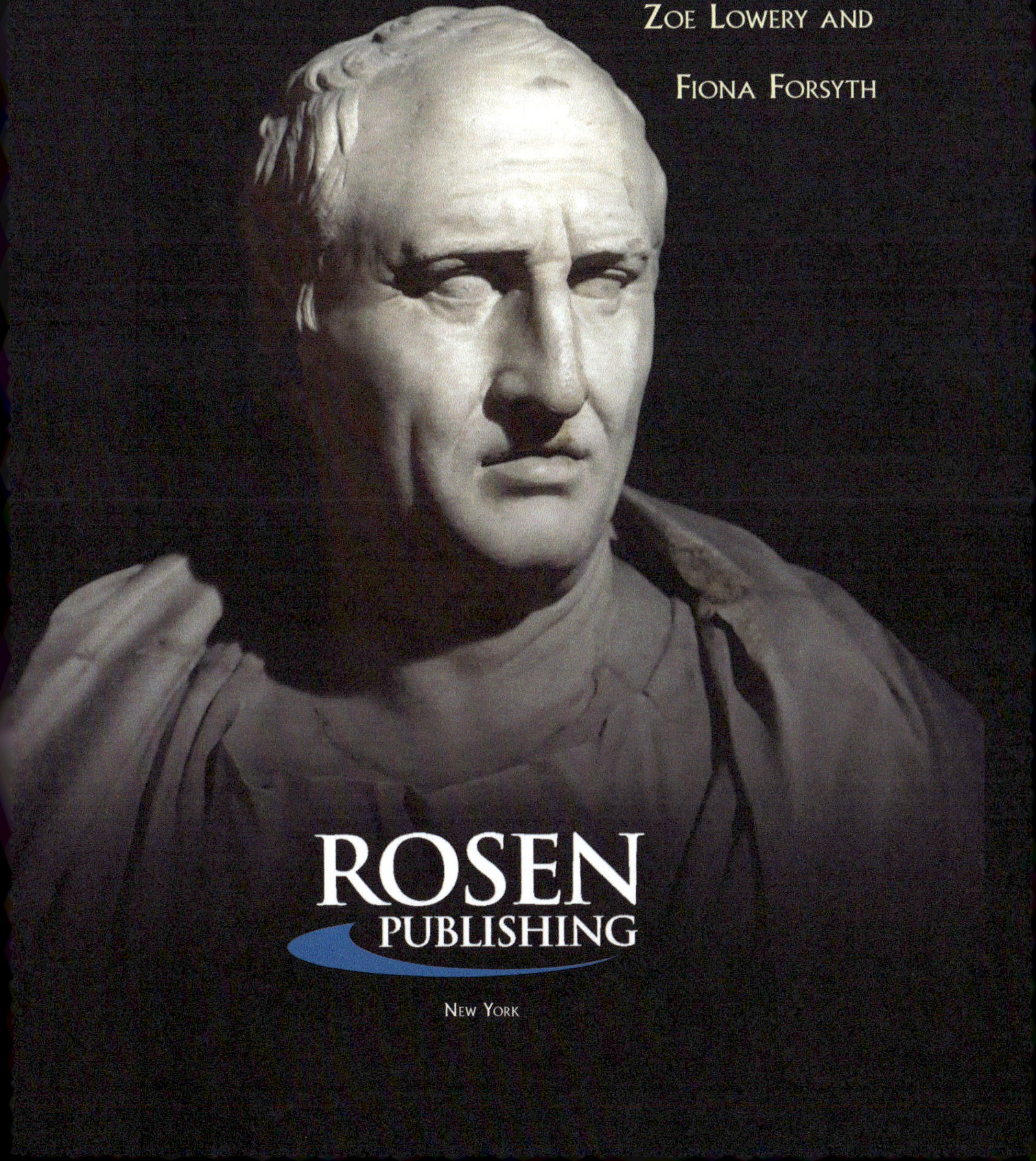

ROSEN PUBLISHING

New York

Published in 2017 by The Rosen Publishing Group, Inc.
29 East 21st Street, New York, NY 10010

First Edition

Library of Congress Cataloging-in-Publication Data

Names: Lowery, Zoe, author. | Forsyth, Fiona, author.
Title: Cicero / Zoe Lowery and Fiona Forsyth.
Description: First edition. | New York, NY : The Rosen Publishing Group, Inc., 2017. | Series: Leaders of the ancient world | Includes bibliographical references and index. | Audience: Grades 7–12.
Identifiers: LCCN 2016022820 | ISBN 9781508172581 (library bound)
Subjects: LCSH: Cicero, Marcus Tullius—Juvenile literature. | Statesmen—Rome—Biography—Juvenile literature. | Orators—Rome—Biography—Juvenile literature. | Rome—Politics and government—265-30 B.C.—Juvenile literature.
Classification: LCC DG260.C5 L66 2016 | DDC 937/.05092 [B] —dc23
LC record available at https://lccn.loc.gov/2016022820

Manufactured in China

CONTENTS

INTRODUCTION

In the first century BCE, the population of the Roman Empire was made up of millions of people from all kinds of places, such as France, North Africa, and the Middle East. They had little in common except that Rome, Italy's centermost city, ruled them all. Most Romans never even saw the ruling city; however, those who were male, rich, highborn, and well-educated might have been involved in Rome's lively political scene. Women, poor people, and slaves had extremely limited rights and power.

Rome was said to have been founded in 753 BCE and had developed into the Mediterranean's most influential city. Rome's sizable and disciplined army had seized many lands, known as provinces. Roman officials governed the captured provinces and collected taxes, which they sent back to an ever more prosperous and powerful Rome.

Wealth and birth meant a great deal to those living in Rome. The amount of wealth and property a family owned determined its official class. Patricians were people in the wealthiest families, and everyone else was a plebeian.

Marcus Tullius Cicero

Rome was transitioning from republic to empire during the first century BCE. Previously, the wealthiest citizens ruled through the Senate. Now, by way of the armies, numerous men saw prospects to become powerful. As a result, these motivated men fought with each other, which resulted in war for over a half century. Ultimately, one motivated man triumphed over all others and became emperor, or Rome's only leader. An emperor's heir took control when his father died, which established the system of one-man rule.

Augustus was the first such emperor. When he spotted a grandson trying to hide a book he was reading, Augustus confiscated it to read it himself. Soon he returned the book, commenting, "He was a clever man, my child; and he loved his country."

This clever man was Marcus Tullius Cicero, who wrote that and many other books. Three men had ordered his execution: the general Mark Antony; Lepidus, who also controlled a sizable army; and Augustus. During a time of tremendous change, this triumvirate had determined that they should share control of Rome, but to do so first required the elimination of all their rivals. Augustus's fearful grandson would not have known that his grandfather allowed Cicero's name to remain on the execution list or that he also respected Cicero's writing and acknowledged his loyalty to Rome. Cicero's patriotism and literary talent played critical roles in his life and death, and Augustus was one among many who were influenced by him.

Of all ancient Romans, we know more about Cicero than any other, mostly thanks to his own writing. Together with the works of other historians, we can look to his numerous speeches as well as hundreds of letters he wrote. Thanks to these letters, today we can get a fairly robust picture of the life of a Roman politician such as Cicero.

CHAPTER 1

ROME: INSIDE AND OUT

Marcus Tullius Cicero came into the world around 106 BCE. Although he would go on to become Rome's greatest orator, he was not born there. His birth was on the farm belonging to his grandfather, located near the hill town called Arpinum. Arpinum was 70 miles (almost 113 kilometers) from Rome, which required between two and three days of travel.

THE PERKS OF CITIZENSHIP

The people of Arpinum were Roman citizens and had been for a long time, so they were more privileged than many of the people living in Italy at the time. Full Roman citizenship was considered valuable. You had the right to a trial if someone accused you of a crime. You were allowed to vote

Rome's greatest orator was born about 106 BCE, but he was born in the hills of Arpinum, outside of the city of Rome.

A NOTE ON ROMAN NAMES AND DATES

Roman names can be confusing. For example, this book is about Marcus Tullius Cicero, son of Marcus Tullius Cicero, and grandson of Marcus Tullius Cicero. He is called "Cicero" throughout the book, and his brother is referred to as "Quintus."

Furthermore, in translating dates from original sources, this book uses the modern and commonly accepted BCE and CE dates rather than the Roman dates used in the original. It is taken for granted that the reader understands that an ancient Roman writing before the birth of Christ would not have written dates in terms of BCE and CE.

in the elections that were held every year in Rome. You may have also felt that you were a part, however small, of the great Roman Empire. Of course it wasn't that simple. No woman could be a Roman citizen and vote, nor could a slave. Even a freed slave was not allowed all the rights of a Roman citizen. And voting in elections was required if you had the time and money to make the journey to

Even if a slave was freed, as shown here, he or she would never be allowed to vote in Rome.

Rome every year. Theoretically, as a citizen, you could vote to decide who was elected to all the posts of government, even that of the chief priest of the Roman religion. You could vote to decide whether or not a proposal became a law. But Rome was not a democracy because all votes were not equal. You voted with many other people in groups, and the voting power of these groups did not all carry the same weight. Some groups had more people in them than other groups, and some were only for rich people. For example, imagine that the election for the top job, the consulship, is being held, and you join your voting group, which is called a century. You are rich and so is everyone else in your century. The century next to you is composed of many more people, who are not as rich.

The Roman Forum, the remains of which are shown here in 2014, was a place for the public to gather.

Each person in that century will find it much more difficult to make his opinion count.

INSIDE AND OUTSIDE

The people in some places in Italy, such as Arpinum, were given full Roman citizenship as a reward for being helpful to Rome as she had expanded to take over Italy and the rest of the Mediterranean. People of other towns and regions were only given a sort of second-class citizenship, called "Latin status," and much of Italy was even lowlier than that, with the grade "Italian status." These citizenships were less worthwhile than full Roman citizenship because they granted fewer rights and opportunities.

It is easy to see why many people who were born and lived in Rome thought of themselves as being superior to anyone who lived outside Rome. It took a long time for urban Romans to realize how this formed a barrier between the city and the empire, even between the city of Rome and the rest of Italy. At the time of Cicero's birth, this difference in treatment was beginning to irritate those who did not enjoy full citizenship. When Cicero was a teenager, a war broke out over this issue. Someone like Cicero from outside Rome could understand and sympathize with the Italians. He always felt himself to be something of an outsider. He once wrote of Arpinum: "I shall never deny that this is my fatherland, even while the other fatherland is greater and contains this one..."

By "the other fatherland" Cicero meant Rome. He was talking about a kind of dual citizenship. Even someone like Cicero, who spent so much of his life in Rome and was deeply involved in its politics, felt that there was a gap between Rome and the rest of Italy. Having this dual citizenship was both an advantage and a disadvantage for Cicero later in his life. He could understand what it was like to be one of the many respectable people who lived outside Rome, and the support of such people helped him a great deal in his career. Unfortunately, to the upper classes born and bred in Rome, Cicero was never one of them, and one even called him "a foreigner"!

QUINTUS, ATTICUS, AND TIRO

Three people were of special importance to Cicero until the end of his life: his younger brother, Quin-

Cicero and his Friends, Atticus and Quintus, at his Villa at Arpinum, as illustrated by Richard Wilson, shows Cicero with two of his closest friends.

tus; his best friend, Atticus; and a slave called Tiro. As a slave, Tiro would have had none of the rights familiar to us in our own time. Instead, he would have been legally viewed as a piece of property. He would have been just one of the millions of people who, through capture in war or birth to a slave mother, were slaves themselves. There were probably more slaves than free people in Rome at this time, and anyone who could afford it would have owned at least one slave. Slavery was a part of Roman life. But a slave and a free citizen could form real bonds of affection, as shown in this letter from Cicero to Tiro:

> The messenger told me that you were now free from fever and getting better, but because he said that you were not

> able to write to me, I got worried—
> and all the more because Hermia,
> who was supposed to arrive that day,
> did not. I really am very concerned
> about your health. Apply your
> considerable intelligence to getting
> yourself well again for me as well as
> for yourself. Once more—take the
> greatest care of yourself.

Eventually, Tiro was officially freed by his friend Cicero, and he would go on to be known as Marcus Tullius Tiro. He continued to be Cicero's friend as well as his secretary.

CHAPTER 2

A ROMAN EDUCATION

A young Roman boy, like Cicero or his brother Quintus, from an established, wealthy family would be sent to a school or have his own tutor at home. He would be taught to read and write Latin and then Greek so that he could appreciate the great literature of the world. The Romans had conquered Greece in the second century BCE and had grown to appreciate the culture and arts of that land so much that the poet Horace later said, "Greece captured her captor." Greek works of art were popular in Roman houses, and Greek literature was considered part of the basic curriculum for young Romans. So Cicero and Quintus would have learned, by heart, large portions of the works of the poet Homer, the man who composed the *Iliad* and the *Odyssey*, long epic poems telling of the Trojan War and the adventures

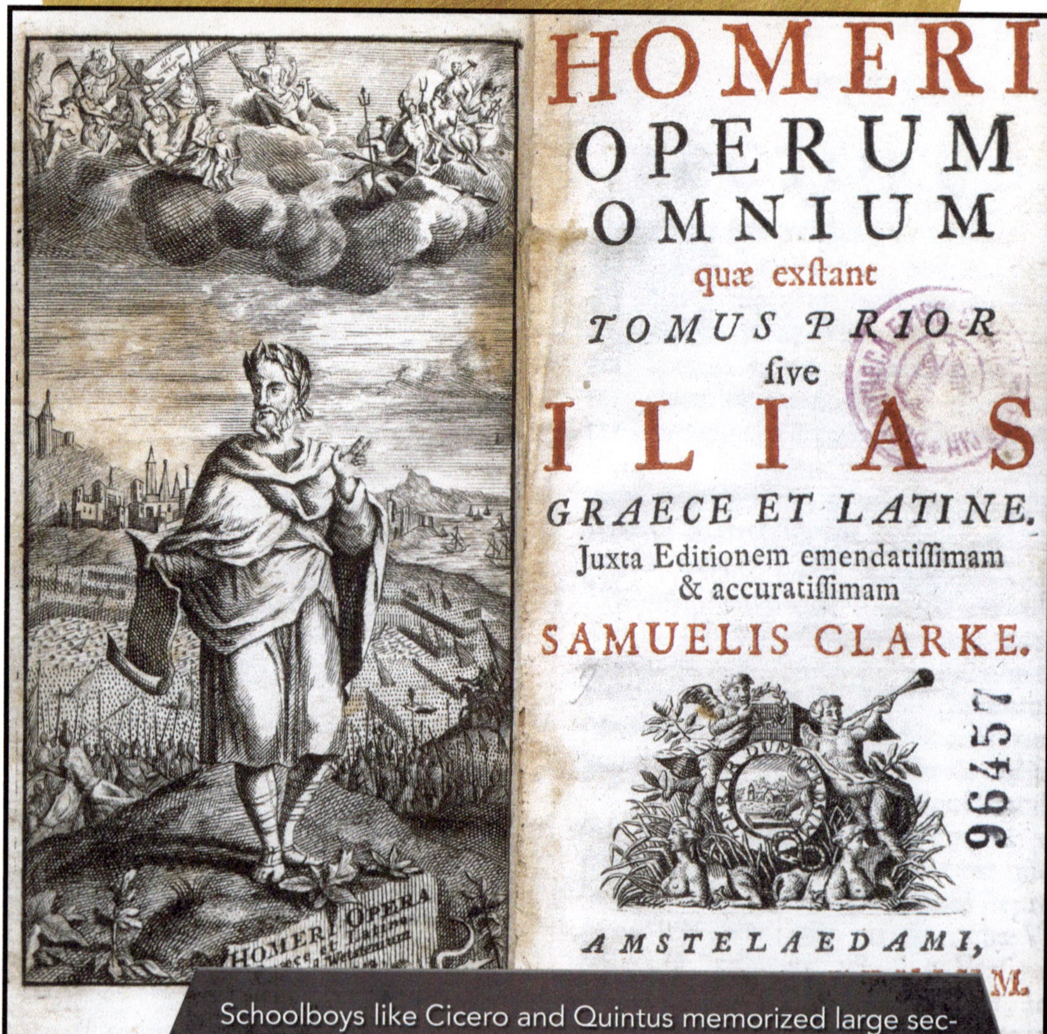

HOMERI
OPERUM
OMNIUM
quæ exſtant
TOMUS PRIOR
ſive
ILIAS
GRAECE ET LATINE.
Juxta Editionem emendatiſſimam
& accuratiſſimam
SAMUELIS CLARKE.

AMSTELAEDAMI,

Schoolboys like Cicero and Quintus memorized large sections of the works and poetry of Homer, such as the *Iliad*.

of the Greek hero Odysseus on his way home from that war. Cicero was inspired by Homer's tales of heroes who placed honor before everything else, and he later wrote to Quintus—using the words of

Achilles, the great hero of the *Iliad*, who died rather than face a life without glory—of "that determination, which I have clung to since I was boy, *to be the best by far, to outreach the rest*."

Cicero and his brother studied the great playwrights, historians, and philosophers of Greece, and Cicero became interested in philosophy. He would write many philosophical works himself later in his life. "Philosophy" comes from a Greek word meaning "love of wisdom." Ancient philos-

LIMITS OF EDUCATION

Education was taken seriously in the Roman world, as long as there was money to pay for it. For a family like Cicero's, education was a lengthy business, lasting until the boy was about seventeen and then continuing if he showed that he had talent. Girls might be taught basic skills such as reading and writing, but it was unusual for a girl to receive any formal education beyond that. The main roles for women in the ancient world were the production of a male heir for her husband and the smooth management of the household.

ophers tried to work out answers to some crucial questions, such as “What is goodness?” or “What is the best way to rule a country?” Cicero was a good student, according to the biographer Plutarch. Plutarch relates the following story from Cicero’s school days: “When he was old enough to go to school, he gained quite a reputation with the other boys, to the point where their fathers began coming to the school because they wanted to see for themselves this Cicero and his renowned grasp of his lessons…”

THE POET AND ORATOR

Plutarch also tells us that Cicero became especially good at two things: poetry and oratory. Cicero’s poetry has not been preserved apart from one or two lines, but it is no surprise to find that he was good at oratory from an early stage. Oratory is the art of making speeches, and Cicero was considered one of the best orators Rome ever had. This becomes even more significant knowing how highly the Romans thought of good speeches.

Today’s media prefer a politician to make their statements short, punchy, and entertaining.

Romans viewed things differently. The ability to make long and intricate speeches was vital to anyone who wanted to make a success of himself in public life. When a politician wanted to get into office, he needed to persuade people to vote for him. If he made good speeches in public places where many people could hear him, his name would become known to a wide audience.

Another way of making a name for oneself before going into politics was to have a career as a lawyer. Any Roman citizen could initiate a prosecution. Indeed, many Romans thought it was their duty to take someone who was breaking the law to court. There was no police force or public prosecutor, and so it was left to individuals to conduct the cases for both the prosecution and defense. Lawyers were also supposed to do this for no other reward than the pleasure of having played their part in upholding the law. In Roman trials, as in modern ones, lawyers for the prosecution and defense had to cross-examine witnesses and make speeches to persuade the jury. Trials were always held in public, so many Romans would attend out of interest, and a lawyer who made entertaining speeches would be noticed by everybody.

Students learned an important skill known as rhetoric in school, which is a manner of persuasive speech or writing.

Schoolboys were taught how to make speeches and how to phrase their speeches in such a way as to persuade people to do what the orator wanted. This skill is called rhetoric, and it is still important today.

Very little in the way of mathematics, geography, or science was taught, but when a boy was

about fifteen he would often receive advanced lessons in philosophy and rhetoric, as well as some practical experience as an apprentice to someone already at the height of his career. Cicero probably received most of his education in Rome, and we do know that he, his father, and his brother,

Quintus, moved to a house in Rome to ensure that the boys could benefit from being in the big city. Cicero was introduced to an experienced lawyer so that he could learn from watching and listening to him. This lawyer was called Scaevola; however, he was old and died during Cicero's time in Rome. His cousin, also called Scaevola, then took on Cicero. Being in a circle of such great men and their friends meant that Cicero would have met other lawyers, writers, and politicians.

At this time Cicero met the person who would become his best and lifelong friend, and the person to whom he addressed most of his letters, Titus Pomponius Atticus. Links between the Pomponius and Tullius Cicero families were to be strengthened even further when Quintus, Cicero's brother, married Atticus's sister Pomponia.

Another possible path for a young man on the rise was that of military service. Though it was not compulsory in times of peace, many families considered a year or so in the army to be useful for a young man. This did not mean that a wealthy young man joined the ranks of the ordinary soldiers. He would instead be attached to the staff of an experienced general and would learn about commanding men and about the practicalities of controlling Rome's empire.

In the Roman army, even the ordinary soldiers were well-paid volunteers and Roman citizens, which meant that no one was forced to join and that every soldier had an interest in keeping the Roman Empire safe and secure. The army was divided into legions of about 5,000 men each. They could be posted anywhere in the empire, to help the governors put down rebellions in their provinces or to carry out attacks on hostile states on the empire's borders.

SULLA'S ASCENT

In Cicero's times, there were such frequent wars, both abroad and in Italy, that a man was lucky to avoid getting involved in conflict. In 91 BCE, while Cicero was still young, a war broke out between Rome and her Italian allies, who wanted greater recognition from Rome. From 89 to 88 BCE, Cicero served on the staff of two generals, Pompeius Strabo and Sulla. This experience, while it does not appear to have brought out any enthusiasm for being a soldier, may have

The Roman General Sulla argued with another general, Marius, and ended up leaving Rome to fight in the Mediterranean Sea.

been useful in introducing Cicero to a wider circle of people. Pompeius Strabo had a son the same age as Cicero, and it is quite possible that the two met during this time. That son was later to be called Magnus, "the Great One," or Pompey the Great. Also on Strabo's staff was a young noble called Lucius Sergius Catiline, who became one of Cicero's greatest enemies.

Rome's war with her allies lasted until 87 BCE, but once the Italian allies were subdued, two great generals, Marius and Sulla, started quarreling with each other. While Sulla went to the eastern end of the Mediterranean Sea to fight King Mithridates, Marius came to power in Rome and managed to get rid of some of his personal enemies before dying of natural causes. For three years, Rome had an uneasy peace, knowing that when Sulla came back from dealing with Mithridates, it was unlikely that he would be willing to forgive and forget his dispute with Marius. During this time, Cicero was in Rome, carrying on his studies under the famous Greek teachers Philon and Diodotus, and he was sure to have picked up on all the political under-currents and learned of his elders' concerns about the situation. No one of influence or power could count themselves safe. Cicero wisely kept out of the

When Sulla returned in 83 BCE, he announced that he would be dictator, effectively giving himself power over every Roman citizen.

limelight, preferring to carry on his studies rather than try to make a dramatic entrance into public life. That was yet to come.

Sulla's return in 83 BCE brought with it the miserable experiences people expected. Not only did Sulla mercilessly seek power, efforts that had the support of a sizable and powerful army, but he declared himself dictator. This brash move provided him power over all Romans. This act was also eye-opening for Cicero, showing him the results of a brutal ruler who took his power by force. The unrest that was caused by Sulla's regime took the lives of Cicero's teacher, Scaevola, and his cousin, Gratidianus.

CHAPTER 3

CICERO'S CAREER COMMENCES

Although his return was characterized by violence, Sulla had a specific plan for the transformation of Rome's politics. One goal was a stronger Senate, which he felt would help work get done with speed and efficiency. Sulla also hoped to change the methods of the legal system, such as by setting up permanent courts to deal with crimes of some kinds.

Unfortunately, Sulla's ruthlessness led to some dark times in Rome. He had a particularly feared way of getting rid of people whom he thought stood in his way—proscription. Sulla would write out a list of those he wanted to get rid of, and the list would be posted at the Forum in the heart of Rome. As this was the place where the law courts, markets, temples, and

Sulla wrote out a list of people he wanted to get rid of and had it posted in Rome's Forum. Here the people check the list for their names.

Senate House were all clustered together, many people in Rome would pass through it each day. Crowds would gather to read the notices to find out whose name was on the dreaded list. High rank and noble birth were of little help if your name was proscribed. A reward was offered to those who carried out the execution of the proscribed person. It gave some people a chance to earn a gruesome living, and others the chance to indulge in personal revenge. Quintus Cicero vividly describes his cousin Marcus Marius Gratidianus' murder by proscription: "...while Marius was still alive and standing, [his killer] used his right hand to cut off the head with a sword, while his left hand held onto the head. He carried the head in his hand, while between his fingers flowed streams of blood."

Ruthless people used these terrifying times to their own advantage. In 80 BCE, a young man called Roscius was accused of killing his own father, a terrible crime called parricide by the Romans. If found guilty, Roscius could have lost all his inheritance and faced possible execution. Cicero decided that the time had come for a dramatic entry into the world of the Roman law

In Cicero's dramatic entrance into the world of Roman law, he successfully argued that Roscius's murder had been thanks to two of his own relatives and a friend of Sulla.

courts and so he defended Roscius. He caused a sensation. Not only did he successfully argue that his client's father had been murdered on the orders of two unscrupulous cousins, he also implicated an ex-slave, a Greek called Chrysogonus. The sensational thing was that Chrysogonus had once belonged to Sulla himself and was still a great friend of the dictator. Cicero had risked offending the most powerful man in Rome in his first important lawsuit! The prosecution had relied on the young and inexperienced Cicero to be so scared of Sulla that he could not defend his client properly.

Cicero, however, was careful to absolve Sulla of any involvement in the case, while attacking Chrysogonus fiercely. This clever tactic allowed the jurors to find Roscius not guilty and show their disapproval of the ex-slave without offending his former master. Later in life, Cicero said that he received a lot of praise for this defense speech and many requests for more speeches: "And so I gave many more speeches, on which I toiled carefully and perhaps a bit too obviously!"

Cicero was being modest, for although his early speeches, like the Roscius speech, were a little florid, they were still good speeches. The Roscius case was also important for Cicero in that it showed him what he still needed by way of training to become a successful speaker. He traveled to Greece to find the teaching and advice he needed. It was probably also a good idea for him to take a break from Rome to let things settle down after his dramatic early success. He was also approaching the age when a young man would be thinking of running for election to the Senate, and he needed to be in top form for that.

STARTING IN THE SENATE

To get into the Senate, a man had to be elected by the people of Rome to the lowest office of what was called the *cursus honorum*, the series of jobs that led you higher and higher in Roman politics. If you wanted to become consul, the highest post in the government, you had to have held both the quaestorship and the praetorship first. The aedileship was useful but not necessary. Another job held by many senators was that of *tribunus plebis*, "tribune of the people." Ten tribunes were elected every year, and their task was to keep an eye on the

At the Curia Julia, one of the Roman Senate Houses, Roman citizens elected a man into a low office, the first in a series of ever-more-prestigious jobs, or *cursus honorum*.

interests of the people of Rome. To do this, they had gained some very strong powers. A tribune was able to propose a law and get a vote held on that law without having to consult the Senate first. He could also stop the Senate from discussing anything if he so wished. This was called the power of the veto. It placed the tribunes in a strange position. They were members of the Senate, and yet they frequently clashed with the Senate in performing their jobs.

Elections were held in the summer before the job had to be taken up, and voting took place on the Campus Martius (the Field of Mars), an area outside the old walls of Rome, where once the men of Rome had done their military training. In the summer of 76 BCE, Cicero went to the Campus Martius and got elected as one of the quaestors for the next year. This was his official entry into the Senate of Rome, of which he would be a member for the rest of his life.

SUCCESS IN SICILY

As a junior member of the government, Cicero's job was to help the governor of Sicily. He went off

CLIMBING THE LADDER: THE *CURSUS HONORUM*

Minimum Age	Number	What Did They Do?
Quaestor		
30	20	Assisted senior officials in a province or in a treasury
Aedile		
37	4	Supervised public services like sewers and roads; organized public entertainment
Praetor		
40	8	Supervised one of the permanent law courts; after a year of office governed a small province
Consul		
43	2	Supervised Senate meetings, elections, and foreign affairs, and were responsible for Rome's security; after a year of office governed a large province

to Sicily to a town called Lilybaeum (now called Marsala) and seems to have both enjoyed himself and worked hard. He described his work there as follows: "I had acquired a large amount of grain at a time when it was very dear, I had been pleasant to the business community, fair to the merchants, generous to the public contractors, unbiased to the allies…"

The young Cicero was pleased with himself, but he was disappointed upon his return because few people had heard of him or his work:

> And so I left the province in the expectation that the people of Rome would hand everything over to me. But as it turned out, when I was in Puteoli on my journey back from the province, it was the season when very many of the wealthiest people are usually there, and you could have knocked me down with a feather when someone asked me when I had left Rome and whether there was any news from the city. When I told him that I was actually on my way back from my province, "Oh

> yes," he said, "Africa, right?" Pretty annoyed, I said in lofty fashion, "No, Sicily." At which, a real know-it-all said "Don't you know anything? He was quaestor at Syracuse." What can one say? I got off my high horse and melted into the crowd of visitors.

But Sicily did more for Cicero than provide him with a good story. It led to another successful lawsuit. In 70 BCE, Cicero was campaigning to be elected aedile, the next post up in the *cursus honorum*. That same year, the people of Sicily sent representatives to Rome to ask for help from the consul, Pompey the Great. They complained that the man who had been governing Sicily for the last three years had been cruel and greedy and they wanted someone to help them prosecute him. They also asked Cicero for help, remembering what a hard-working and honest quaestor he had been when he had worked in Sicily. Cicero took the case, and the ex-governor, Verres, was charged with extortion.

Cicero was up against some strong vested interests. Verres had some powerful friends in the Senate who started to work on his behalf. Verres's allies tried delaying tactics. Cicero traveled to Sic-

Pompey the Great

ily and collected witnesses and evidence as fast as he could. He was back in Rome before anyone expected him.

Cicero opened the trial in the summer of 70 BCE with such a scorching speech for the prosecution that Verres slinked out of Rome that very night. He fled to Marseilles in southern France, leaving behind a triumphant Cicero. This huge accomplishment commenced his aedileship with a reputation as a man who defended right against might. Cicero's career was off to a magnificent start.

CHAPTER 4

CICERO AND THE CONSPIRATORS

One of Cicero's responsibilities as aedile was to supervise Rome's markets. "When Cicero was aedile," explained Plutarch, "the Sicilians, to show their gratitude, sent him lots of the island's produce. He made no personal profit out of this, but used the favor to lower market prices as much as he could." Cicero continued to work as a lawyer, while organizing the public entertainment for Roman festivals.

HARD WORK AND SUCCESS

The praetorship was Cicero's next step, and he achieved it confidently in 66 BCE. "Three times," he explained, "thanks to the elections being postponed, I was elected praetor at the top of the polls by all the voting groups."

As praetor, he was in charge of the law court that tried cases of extortion—the very charge that had been brought against Verres four years earlier.

Cicero also made a crucial political decision in 66 BCE. He supported a move to give a special mission to Pompey the Great. Pompey was currently engaged in getting rid of the pirates who infested the Mediterranean Sea and who had interfered with Roman trade to the point that the price of goods that were transported by sea increased greatly. It was proposed that Pompey should now be sent to Asia, with the job of finishing a war that Rome had been fighting with King Mithridates for years. Mithridates was king of a region called Pontus, near the Black Sea, and he had overrun the Roman province of Asia in 88 BCE, sparking off the war that Sulla had fought before becoming dictator. Twenty years later, Mithridates was still a threat. The senators' feelings were mixed. Mithridates needed to be dealt with, but should such resources and powers be given to a man like Pompey? The Senate was worried that he might start acting like another dictator. Cicero, however, argued that Pompey was the only man to do the job that had to be done. Pompey did get the special mission, and he defeated Mithridates in three years.

King Mithridates was responsible for triggering the war in Pontus, and remained a threat even twenty years later.

Of course, having Rome's greatest general on his side just before he started his campaign for the

FAMILY LIFE

By now, Cicero had married and had a daughter, Tullia. His wife, Terentia, was wealthy and came from a respectable upper-class Roman family. Making the right marriage was crucial for a politician. His wife had to be from the right sort of family. Roman women were expected to bring a dowry—an amount of property or money—to the marriage, and a wife's relatives could be useful allies in political life. When aiming for the top, every opportunity had to be exploited.

consulship, the highest office of state, was useful to Cicero. Cicero was determined to be consul, despite the fact that he was what was called a *novus homo*, Latin for "new man." This meant that no one from his family had held the consulship or even been in the Senate before him. It was rare for a new man to earn the consulship. How was Cicero going to achieve his aim? To begin with, he checked out his fellow candidates. In a letter to Atticus written in 65 BCE, a year before Cicero planned to stand as a candidate himself, he wrote:

> "The ones I am sure of are Galba, Antonius, and Cornificius. I imagine you are either laughing or groaning at him! And you'll have to pinch yourself when you hear that there are some who think that Caesonius will run! For I do not think Aquillius will run, because he has actually denied it, and he has put in a plea of illness, and his reign over the law courts is in the way. Catiline will certainly be in the running, as long as his trial decides that there is no light at mid-day. I don't suppose you are holding your breath for me to write about Aufidius and Palicanus."

Of the men mentioned in this extract, only Antonius and Catiline proved to be serious contenders. Cicero actually considered defending Catiline in the trial he mentions, but for some reason changed his mind.

Not long after this letter was written, Cicero's son Marcus was born. It must have seemed to Cicero that everything was going well. He now had a son and heir, which probably did him no harm with the electorate. To the Romans, sons were important, as they would carry on the family name and keep the family's property together.

The next thing a candidate had to do was to get down to some good, hard canvassing for votes. A little handbook of election campaigning, supposedly written by Quintus to his brother, has survived from that time. It is full of tips on how to get votes. Some tips sound as though they might be useful in a modern political campaign:

> The word "friend" is used more widely in an election campaign than in any other aspect of life. Anyone who shows you any goodwill, anyone who seeks you out, anyone who calls at your house, is to be called a friend.
>
> People from the market towns and countryside think they are our friends if we just know their names.
>
> You have to use flattery, which even though it is considered a failing and distasteful in other

> aspects of life, is still necessary in an election campaign.
>
> Men don't just want promises; they want grand and flattering promises.
>
> Make sure that gossip gets around, suited to each of your competitors' characters, regarding their misdeeds, scandals, and bribery.

Cicero certainly knew how to blacken the characters of his opponents, going as far as to accuse Catiline of trying to overthrow the state! Romans were allowed to speak much more freely against their opponents without fear of libel lawsuits. The art of invective—insulting someone—was much admired.

His hard work paid off, and in the summer of 64 BCE Cicero was elected consul. He took up office on January 1, 63 BCE. His fellow consul was Antonius, with whom Cicero seems to have made a deal. In return for keeping out of Cicero's way during the year, Antonius got the job of governing an important province the year after. As it turned out, this was a good deal, for Antonius kept his side of the bargain throughout an eventful year.

A LIFE-CHANGING MISTAKE

Cicero ran an effective spy service as consul and used his spies to keep a close eye on Catiline, the man who had hoped to be one of the consuls. It seemed that he was not taking his defeat in a graceful way, and Cicero soon suspected that Catiline was going to try to take over Rome in a rebellion. Cicero set about trying to gather proof, but it was not easy. He watched the men who were Catiline's friends and recruited an "insider," the girlfriend of one of these men, as an informer. Fulvia would ask her boyfriend, Curius, what was going on and then secretly report back to Cicero. She could not, however, give testimony in a trial. She was a woman, for one thing, and it is unlikely that many Roman senators would have taken her seriously.

Cicero kept watch on Catiline and listened for news outside Rome. As he had feared, there were soon rumors of armed men gathering in the north, in the part of Italy called Etruria. In November, he moved against Catiline, accusing him in a meeting of the Senate of being the mastermind of a fiendish plot against Rome. Catiline denied it hotly, but that night he left Rome and went straight to a place

Cicero's First Oration Against Catiline, illustrated by Tancredi Scarpelli, shows him in the act of delivering a scathing accusation that accuses Catiline of attempting to overthrow the state.

Cicero Denounces Catiline, illustrated by Cesare Maccari. Cataline denied the accusations, but that night he crept out of Rome in the dark.

north of Rome called Faesulae, where he joined up with a man called Manlius, who had been in charge of gathering the armed men. The timid Senate at last moved. They declared Catiline a public enemy, and one army was sent to deal with him and Manlius in the north, while another army went south to make sure that no sympathetic southern Italians decided to join in the rebellion. Cicero now turned his attention back to Rome.

Several of Catiline's supporters had been left in Rome, but Cicero did not have any proof of who they were until they played into his hands. He was told about some Gauls from a tribe called the Allobroges who happened to be in Rome on business. They had been secretly approached by men claiming to be Catiline's lieutenants and had been asked to persuade their tribe to join in the rebellion. Cicero asked the Allobroges to play along and persuade the conspirators to give them letters to take back to their tribe. This they did, and the conspirators fell for it. One of them, a man called Volturcius, decided to go with the Allobroges as far as Catiline's camp, where he would deliver a letter to Catiline. On the morning of December 3, 63 BCE, the Gauls and Volturcius left Rome, taking the Mulvian Bridge over the Tiber. Cicero takes up the story:

> And so I summoned the praetors Flaccus and Pomptinus, brave men and true patriots. I told them the story and showed them what they must do. But they, feeling all that noble patriots should, without argument and without hesitation took

over, and as evening drew near, made their way in secret to the Mulvian Bridge, and there lay in wait in two separate houses nearby, the Tiber and its bridge between them. Without arousing suspicion they had led many brave men there, and I had sent several armed men from the town of Raete, selected young men whom I often use in the defence of the Republic. In the meantime, the third watch of the night was almost over, when the ambassadors of the Allobroges and their party, Volturcius with them, began to cross the bridge. The ambush fell; swords were drawn by their men and ours. The whole affair was known only to the praetors; everyone else was in the dark. Then Pomptinus and Flaccus intervened, and the fight which had started died down. All the letters found there were handed over to the praetors with the seals still unbroken; the men themselves, under

> arrest, were brought to me as the day was dawning.

Those letters changed everything, condemning five important Romans, including a praetor, Lentulus, after their letters were read in the Senate on December 4. The Senate praised Cicero, Pomptinus, and Flaccus for their work. It took two days for the Senate to decide on the arrested conspirators' fates, but they finally decreed that they should be executed. Although he was left without any other choice, putting the five conspirators to death on the night of December 5 would turn out to be one of the worst mistakes of Cicero's career.

CHAPTER 5

THE CONSEQUENCES OF CICERO'S ACTIONS

As the man who saved Rome and was graced with the title, *pater patriae*, "father of his country," by a grateful Senate, Cicero's consulship appeared to be ending on a high note. Because so many people had cooperated to overthrow Catiline's threat, Cicero began to endorse the idea of all of Rome's classes working together, or *concordia ordinum*. Not everyone was as enthusiastic about this blend of classes, though.

A GRAVE MISTAKE

As a lawyer, Cicero should have foreseen the big problem. Under Roman law, every Roman citizen had the right to a trial. The five men executed on December 5, 63 BCE, were not given their trial, and objections were raised even before Cicero left office

Cicero, painted by Giusto di Gand, decided to leave office on December 31, but he was blocked from making the traditional speech.

on December 31. Traditionally, on that date the outgoing consul would make a speech. But Cicero found himself blocked. The new tribunes of the people had come into office on December 10, and one of them refused to allow Cicero to make a speech on the grounds that he had executed Romans citizens without a trial. No one took it any further for the moment, but Cicero knew that this made him vulnerable. This caused him to make another mistake. He was so insecure that he kept reminding everyone that he had saved Rome. His biographer Plutarch writes, "There wasn't a Senate meeting, an assembly of the people, or a lawsuit without one having to listen to him babbling on about Catiline and Lentulus."

The armies sent out by the Senate caught up with the rebels north of Rome, and in February of 62 BCE, Catiline died along with his rebellion on the battlefield. Cicero went on with his legal work and bought an expensive new house on the Palatine Hill, overlooking the Forum where he had made so many speeches in the Senate House and law courts. Pompey had also finished the war against Mithridates in the East, and everyone was waiting for the Great One to come back to Rome in triumph.

THE CLODIUS CONTROVERSY

And at the end of 62 BCE, there arose another scandal, which at first appeared to have nothing to do with Cicero. He casually refers to it in a letter to Atticus: "I suppose that you have heard that Publius Clodius was caught dressed in women's clothes in the house of Caesar when the sacrifice for the safety of the people was taking place, and that he only got out safe thanks to a slave girl. It's a huge scandal, which I know will upset you."

The sacrifice referred to was the Rite of the Good Goddess, a festival celebrated only by women. It was a sacrilege for a man to witness the rites. When Publius Clodius Pulcher, a notoriously mischievous young aristocrat, was rumored to have been discovered at the festival dressed as a woman, many Romans were horrified. Clodius was brought to trial and only through a massive bribery effort was acquitted. But he was not pleased with the person who challenged his alibi at that trial, Marcus Tullius Cicero, who testified that he had seen Clodius in Rome that day. It made Clodius's defense—that he had been miles away from Rome at the time—look a bit thin. From then on, Clodius did not like Cicero and his family. Plutarch adds a fascinating story to explain why Cicero got involved at all: "It seemed that Cicero gave evidence, not out of desire for the truth, but to defend himself against his wife Ter-

SIDEBAR CONTINUED ON PAGE 66

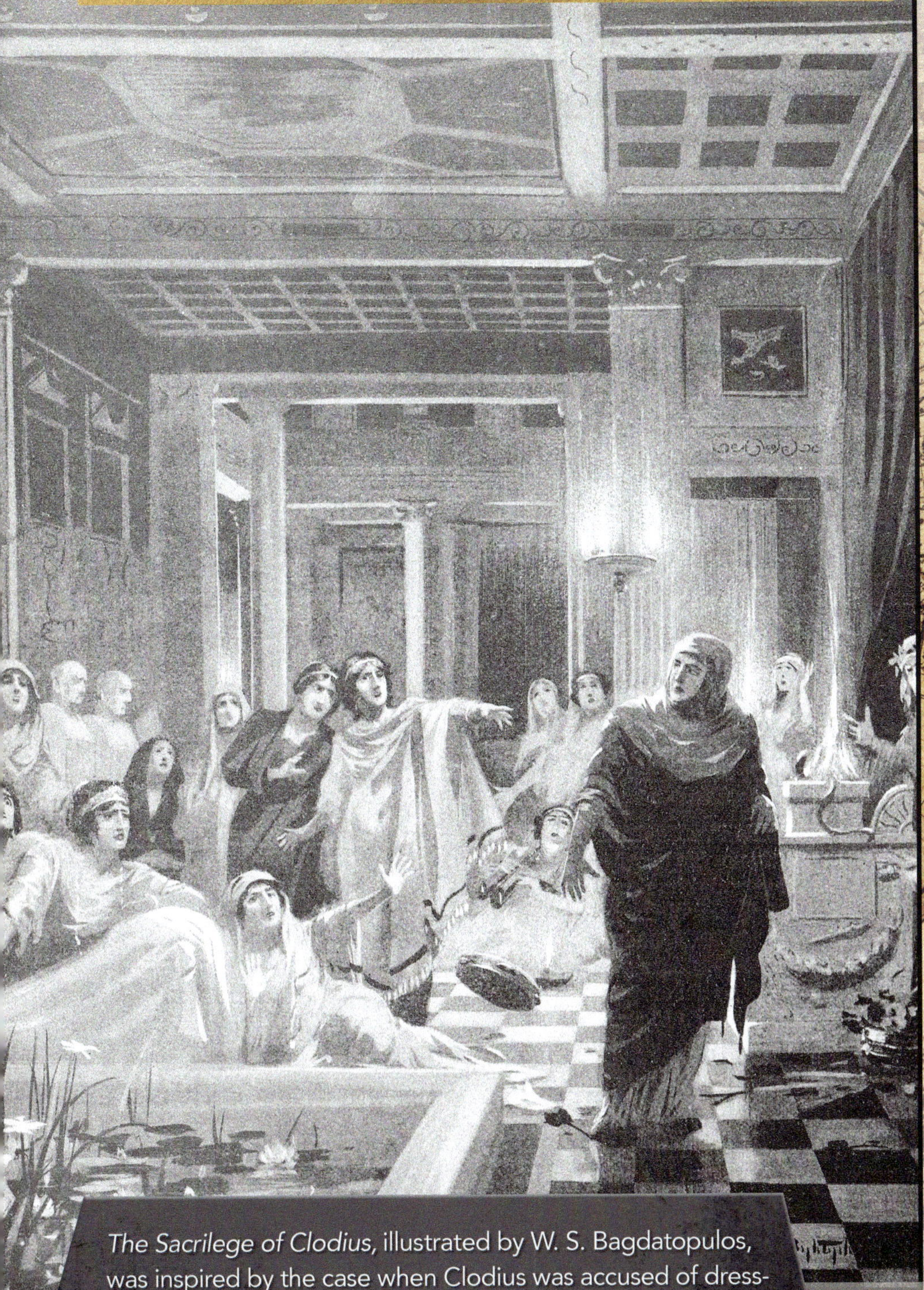

The Sacrilege of Clodius, illustrated by W. S. Bagdatopulos, was inspired by the case when Clodius was accused of dressing like a woman and sneaking into a female-only festival.

SIDEBAR CONTINUED FROM PAGE 64

entia. She did not like Clodius because of his sister Clodia, whom she suspected of wanting to marry Cicero… Terentia was an awkward woman and had a great deal of influence over Cicero so she provoked him into joining her in the attack and testifying against Clodius.

Roman women had fewer rights at that time. They could not vote, for example. But Terentia reminds us that women had a great deal of influence over their husbands. If Plutarch is correct, her jealousy had a far-reaching effect.

POMPEY, CRASSUS, AND CAESAR: THE TRIUMVIRATE

For the moment, though, Cicero had more serious matters to concern him. At the beginning of 59 BCE, he and other Romans found themselves in a dilemma. For various reasons, mainly having to do with sheer exasperation with the Senate, Julius

Caesar had formed an alliance with Pompey the Great and a man called Crassus in 60 BCE. The three of them had wealth, military might, and ambition, and they decided to combine all their resources so that they could ensure that each member of the pact got what he wanted without having to go through the usual slow channels. Caesar was elected consul in 59 BCE, and when he was in power the three men used his office so they were able to run Rome however they pleased. The Senate, naturally, was outraged, and so was Cicero. Additionally, he was upset that Pompey, a man he admired greatly, was a member of this gang of three.

At first the three men tried to get Cicero on their side, but he refused. When he started speaking out against them, they decided to muzzle him and chose Publius Clodius as their agent. For some time, Clodius had been trying to get the office of tribune of the people. Pompey, Crassus, and Caesar supported Clodius, and their support was enough to get him elected. Cicero began to get worried. Suppose Clodius tried to pass a law against him? This was of course what Clodius intended to do. He became tribune at the end of 59 BCE, and when the new consuls came into power on January 1, 58 BCE, Clodius was able to get them on his side by giving them good provinces to govern. They did not interfere for the rest of the year. It was the exact same trick as Cicero had pulled back in 63 BCE with his fellow consul, Antonius.

EXILE

Cicero started rallying his supporters, but unfortunately he was out of favor. Everyone was fed up with hearing him go on so much about Catiline. He went to see Pompey, but Pompey conveniently managed to slip out of the back door at the exact same time as Cicero came in the front. Cicero was in a state of despair. After consulting with his friends, he left Rome under the cover of night, just like his old enemies Verres and Catiline, and went to Greece before Clodius could move against him.

In fact, Clodius's suggested law would exile anyone who did not provide Roman citizens with a trial before they were put to death. So Cicero's recent actions in 63 BCE offered Clodius the

Julius Caesar

perfect opening. Clodius was able to to pass the law, and even though Cicero had already left Rome, Clodius had Cicero's house demolished. In its place he built a Temple to Liberty. He hoped would serve as a reminder to all who saw it that he believed Cicero had failed to defend liberty in 63 BCE when he sent the Catiline conspirators to their deaths without the benefit of a trial.

CHAPTER 6

ROME DIVIDED

Clodius did not stop with the destruction of Cicero's home. He devastated Cicero's country houses. He assaulted Quintus, Cicero's brother, and abandoned his wounded body in the Forum. Clodius even passed bills that gave him the right to form crews that offered free grain to Rome's poorest. Such generosity was popular with some, but those in power were not impressed. He was beyond the control of Pompey and Crassus, who remained in Rome. Julius Caesar had left after his consulship to govern Gaul, a province in present-day France.

The decision to recall Cicero was made in 57 BCE, but it still took more time than Cicero would have liked. Exile was the low point of his life. Reading his letters, it appears that he was not capable of bearing his troubles without an unremitting stream of woe, such as in this letter to Quintus:

> "My brother, my brother, my brother, were you really worried that out of anger I had sent my people to you with no letter? Or that I didn't want to see you? Angry with you? Could I be angry with you? Oh yes, of course, it's you who have hurt me, your enemies and the dislike felt for you which have destroyed me, not I that have pitiably harmed you! That praised consulship of mine has snatched you, my children, my country, my fortunes away from me."

In 57 BCE, with Cicero's friend Lentulus Spinther as consul and with Pompey once more Cicero's friend, Clodius could not stop Cicero's return. Along with Lentulus Spinther, three other friends of Cicero's—Sestius, Milo, and Cispius—were tribunes. These four men had worked tirelessly to keep Cicero's case in the public eye and had canvassed on his behalf for nearly fifteen months on end. Sestius had even gone to Gaul to see Julius Caesar and plead for Cicero, and he had been injured along

Cicero's September 7, 57 BCE, speech in the Senate recommended that Pompey be in charge of overseeing the corn supply.

with Quintus in the Forum riot. Cicero was now triumphant, but poor and in debt to a lot of people. He began work almost immediately. On September 7, 57 BCE, he made a speech in the Senate recommending that the supervision of the corn supply be handed over to Pompey. This was a prestigious and powerful position, made necessary because of Clodius's corn dole, which had practically drained the treasury. Cicero then began the fight to get his house back. The Senate turned over the land to Cicero once more, along with 2 million sesterces to rebuild. This was not nearly enough compensation for a house that in 62 BCE had cost him 3.5 million sesterces, but Cicero remained silent about it in public. To Atticus he complained that the senators had been "stingy" when they awarded him 500,000 and 250,000 sesterces for the two country estates destroyed by Clodius's gangs. Cicero was short of money now, and to make things worse, his relationship with his wife was not going well. At the beginning of October, he wrote to Atticus, "The other things that bother me are a bit more private. I am loved by my brother and daughter." Cicero's exclusion of Terentia from this group is obvious.

VENGEANCE!

From November 57 BCE onward, Cicero got caught up in the running battle between Clodius and the tribune Milo. Milo may have been on Cicero's side, but he behaved similarly to Clodius, forming his own bands of thugs and using just as much violence in retaliation. By this time, Clodius was trying to gain the office of aedile, while Milo was using his gangs to provoke riots in order to delay the elections. It was January 56 BCE before the elections were held and Clodius was made aedile. Cicero was kept busy at the start of the year, defending those friends who had fought Clodius when he was in exile. Milo, Sestius, Cispius, and another Cicero supporter, Lucius Bestia, were all charged with one thing or another by cronies of Clodius's during the first three months of 56 BCE.

Then, in April 56 BCE, Cicero took on an interesting case. A young man who had once been Cicero's student, Marcus Caelius Rufus, was charged with violence, theft, and poisoning. The main witness for the defense was going to be Clodius's own sister, Clodia. Cicero made her the target of an abusive speech. It was a wonderful way of gaining revenge on the whole Clodius family. The charges against Caelius were almost lost in the barrage aimed at Clodia:

> "If an unmarried woman opens her home to eager all-comers, and openly lives the life of a prostitute, meeting with men who are complete strangers to her, if this woman does this in the city, in her garden, in the throng at Baiae, if not just the way she walks, but the way she dresses and the company she keeps, not just her come-to-bed eyes, not just her free talk, but also her touch, her kiss, her parties—on the beach, on board her ship, at home…"

For a Roman woman to be held up to public scrutiny like this was a terrible scandal. Caelius was acquitted.

SILENCED

Full of confidence, on April 5, 56 BCE, Cicero

breezed into the Senate and launched an attack on Caesar's legislation. On the eighth of April, he visited Pompey, who told him that he was off to Sardinia to meet with Cicero's brother, Quintus, about the corn supply. Cicero wrote a cheery letter to Quintus to tell him to watch out for the great man's arrival. On the eleventh of April, Pompey set off, but not for Sardinia. He traveled up the coast to Luca, the southernmost town in Gaul, to meet with Caesar and Crassus. The three men were dissatisfied with the way Roman politics were going and decided they needed to step in once more. Among other things, they decided to silence Cicero. Pompey finally made it to Sardinia, and it was probably there that he told Quintus to convey a message to his older brother that Cicero had to keep quiet. Cicero's brief fight ended. Exile was something he did not dare risk again.

OUT OF THE LIMELIGHT

Cicero remained out of Roman politics for the next few years. He kept up his legal work and even appeared to defend men recommended by Caesar, Crassus, and Pompey. He was not proud of what he called his "about-turn," but it showed the three men that he was willing to accept their terms. When Milo finally killed Clodius in a clash on the Appian Way outside Rome, Cicero felt obliged to defend him, but he was so cowed that he made a mess of the speech. Milo became one of Cicero's few legal failures.

Sometime around 53 BCE, something important happened in the private life of the Tullius family. Cicero freed his slave-secretary Tiro, and Quintus wrote a letter of congratulations to him.

Tiro had achieved a new legal status by being freed. There were still some restrictions on him—he could not join the legions of the army, for example—but he was now a Roman citizen.

CAESAR VERSUS POMPEY

Legal work and family matters did not mean that Cicero was unaware of the heightening political tension toward the end of the decade. When Crassus was killed while fighting in Asia, there was no longer anyone to keep the ambitions of Caesar and Pompey from clashing. Caesar and Pompey began to move toward a confrontation. At the crucial moment, chance intervened to send Cicero away. A shortage of suitable senior politicians meant that he had to serve a term as governor of the province of Cilicia in Asia. In 51 and 50 BCE, while he was away, Cicero used Marcus Caelius Rufus to keep him informed. Caelius sent him shrewd letters analyzing the situation and discussing the all-important question: If it came to a war between Caesar and Pompey, how did one choose which side to join? Caelius wrote:

> Regarding the crisis of the republic, as I have often written to you before now, I don't see peace lasting another year, and the nearer the clash which must happen, the clearer the danger. This is the sticking point over which the men in power are drawing up their battle lines. Pompey has decided that Caesar cannot hold the consulship without handing over army and province, while Caesar has decided that it is not possible to leave his army safely; but he offers this con-

> dition—that they both hand over their armies. So their friendship and uneasy agreement has come to this—not a secret bickering but full-blown hostilities. And I cannot see what decision I should take—I dare say that this dilemma will be troubling you as well. On the one hand, I have influence and ties of friendship; on the other I hate the men but love the cause.

When a civil war broke out in 49 BCE, Caelius chose wisely and went over to Caesar. Cicero found the decision much more difficult because he thought both sides were wrong. He tried very hard to act as a peacemaker between the two men, but neither was interested, and so in the end Cicero went with his heart and followed Pompey to Greece and to a decisive battle at Pharsalus. He must have puzzled Pompey's

Cicero ultimately decided to follow Pompey to Greece and the Battle of Pharsalus, although once there he refused to fight.

supporters. He had joined their cause late, found their desire for battle inexplicable, refused to take part in the battle of Pharsalus, and, after the battle, refused to continue fighting. He limped back to Italy as Pompey was fleeing to Egypt. When news came that Pompey had been murdered by the Egyptians as a "present" for Caesar, Cicero fell into despair. One man was now in control of Rome—the sort of rule Cicero had been fighting all his political life, and the complete opposite of his own dream of *concordia ordinum*. He had to wait in Brundisium in southern Italy for Caesar to forgive him for joining the wrong side in the civil war, and it must have been a very anxious wait for him. According to Plutarch, Caesar was generous: "Caesar when he saw Cicero coming to meet him far ahead of the others, got down and greeted him, and went along the road for some distance talking privately with him. And from then on he treated him with honor and kindness."

Although Cicero was allowed back into Rome under Caesar, he felt that he could not participate fully in politics. His Rome did not exist under this dictator.

Most of the time Caesar was away from Rome, wrapping up loose ends and quenching any fires of resistance. In his absence, the Senate did as he directed.

CHAPTER 7

FAREWELLS

During the years of Caesar's dictatorship, not only was Cicero's personal life turbulent, but he also longed to be back in politics. He wrote to Atticus, "What use is a house to me if I can't have the Forum? My life is over, Atticus, and had been over for a long time—it's just that now I admit it, after losing the one thing that kept me holding on." Without politics, life seemed pointless to Cicero.

After his return to Rome, Cicero and Terentia divorced, but he struggled without her. When his daughter died, his grief led him to be rather sharp with his new wife, Publilia. According to Plutarch, she did not share Cicero's grief for Tullia. The young wife could not compete with a stepdaughter who was older than herself and so well-loved. Cicero was not prepared to be understanding, so he divorced Publilia.

Once more his treatment of his wife appears more than a little shabby. One friend who understood how Cicero was feeling was Servius Sulpicius, and he referred to the political situation in his letter of sympathy to Cicero:

> ...If I could have been there with you I would have been where you needed me and I would have told you of my grief in person . . . Why is it that private sorrow should move you so greatly? Think—how has fortune dealt with us lately? All those things that ought to be as dear to us as children, have been seized from us—country, honor, distinction, every reward of service. What can one more loss add to our pain? Or since we have been hardened by such experiences, shouldn't we have thick skins by now and care less about everything? Or is it for her sake that you grieve? How often must you have thought—as I often have—that, in

Servius Sulpicius could commiserate with Cicero's uncomfortable and perhaps intolerable situation with a less-than-empathetic Publilia after Cicero's daughter died.

TROUBLED HEARTS

At the time of their divorce, Cicero and Terentia had been married for about thirty years. Plutarch's account makes it clear that people speculated as to why Cicero and Terentia had split up after so long:

> He divorced his wife Terentia, after suffering her neglect during the war...she emptied Cicero's house of everything and had many large debts besides. These are the most likely reasons given for the divorce, but Terentia denied them, and Cicero himself gave clear corroboration to her by marrying a young girl not long after. According to Terentia he was in love with her youth, but according to what Tiro, Cicero's freedman, wrote, it was because of the opportunity to pay his debts. For the girl was very rich, and Cicero had been made her guardian and trustee of her inheritance. As he owed a lot of money, he was persuaded by friends and family to marry the girl, even at his time of life, and to use her wealth to get rid of his creditors.

It is a familiar story, and Cicero does not come out of it well. The new marriage itself was not destined to last. Cicero's daughter, Tullia, also had been unhappy in her marriage to a wayward young man called Dolabella, and she divorced her husband at the end of 46 BCE. She was pregnant and gave birth in January 45. The birth left her ill, and she died in February. Cicero was heartbroken.

> these times, those who are allowed to exchange life for death have not got the worst of the bargain!

Sulpicius's letter reveals several interesting things about men like Sulpicius and Cicero. They did not feel embarrassed about their feelings and accepted that they should grieve. Their education in Greek philosophy, however, led them to try to put their own troubles into perspective. The political situation was always foremost in their thoughts.

And yet, Caesar's dictatorship cannot be said to have been a complete disaster for Rome. Caesar was an intelligent and resourceful man, and his long years of fighting and command made him used to getting things done efficiently. He carried out many reforms that were of immense benefit to Rome.

Even before Tullia's death, Cicero had embarked on an impressive period of writing. He had composed works on oratory and started a series of translations of Greek works on philosophy. He wanted to form Latin words to express Greek ideas. He went back to writing poetry—up to 500 lines in an evening according to Plutarch—and intended to write a history of Rome.

AFTER THE ASSASSINATION

When Julius Caesar was assassinated on March 15, 44 BCE, Cicero's name was called out by the assassin Marcus Brutus. Cicero answered this call with a return to politics, at the age of sixty-two. The assassins, or liberators as they preferred to be known, had not planned ahead. They had decided to kill Caesar and had thought that things would go back to normal afterward. They had not anticipated the powerful men who came forward to fight over the rule of Rome in Caesar's place—people like Mark Antony, who had been Caesar's right-hand man. There was also Caesar's heir, a nineteen-year-old called Octavian, who turned out to be fiercely ambitious and ruthless.

At first, Cicero watched and waited in some anxiety. He left Rome, intending to visit his son Marcus, who was studying in Greece, but changed his mind. In August 44 BCE, he traveled back to Rome and made ready to join in the debate over what should happen. This was to prove his downfall. He began to criticize Mark Antony and to support the young Octavian, who was later known as Augustus. He made a series of speeches that criticized and infuriated Mark Antony, whose vigorous replies ensured that he and Cicero were to become enemies. Octavian, on the other hand, seemed willing to take Cicero's advice and support. He already had the power of being Julius Caesar's heir—many of Caesar's former soldiers, for example, rallied to him—and he now needed support in the Senate. Plutarch says that Octavian went so far as to call Cicero "father"! Cicero thought that he would be able to use the young Octavian against Antony, but others saw the dangers more clearly. Marcus Brutus, one of the men who assassinated Caesar, could not understand why Cicero was so easily taken in by Octavian. Brutus wrote to Atticus:

> ...But in some respects this man, the
> most careful of all men, has acted

in a way which I could call naive or ingratiating...I have only one thing to say to you, that Cicero has stirred up rather than calmed the boy's greed and waywardness...Let Octa-

vian call Cicero 'father' then, let him consult Cicero in every matter, let him praise and thank him—this will become clear, that he does not mean what he says...

The Death of Julius Caesar was illustrated by Vincenzo Camuccini. Cicero's response to this assassination would prove to be his ruin.

Unfortunately, Brutus was right. Octavian used Cicero's influence in the Senate to achieve a high position for one so young. When the Senate decided to act against Mark Antony, Octavian accompanied the two consuls to the battlefield. When the consuls died during the fighting, Octavian was left in command of the army. If anything had been learned by the Senate in the last fifty years, it was that men who command the loyalty of an army are dangerous. On July 27, 43 BCE, Cicero wrote a letter to Marcus Brutus, and it is clear that he was beginning to realize what Octavian was like: "I hope to hold onto him [Octavian] despite the heavy opposition: he seems to be naturally of the right character, but he's at a dangerous age and there are many people ready to lead him astray."

Octavian was not led astray by anyone. He was his own master. He persuaded Cicero and the Senate that he, Octavian, should receive the consulship at the young age of twenty. Once he had achieved this, he started negotiations with Antony, knowing that Cicero and the Senate were not going to trust him for much longer. Earlier that year, he had heard a rumor that Cicero had described him as "someone to cultivate, elevate, and eliminate."

In November 43 BCE, Octavian and Antony decided to join forces with a third man, Lepidus, and form a triumvirate, a rule of three like that of Caesar, Crassus, and Pompey nearly twenty years before. They drew up a list of people who would have to be disposed of, and Cicero's name was right at the top of the list, at Mark Antony's request. Octavian fought to save Cicero for two days but gave way to Antony on the third day.

Cicero and his brother and nephew heard of the threat and they fled. They set off for Cicero's house at Astura but decided to split up along the way so that Quintus could go to his house and get some of his things. Quintus and his son were caught and killed. Cicero made it to Astura and started sailing down the coast. He had stopped off at one of his houses at a place called Caieta, and some loyal slaves were trying to hurry him down to the sea in a litter when Antony's men, led by a soldier called Herennius, caught up with him. He told the slaves to stop and waited in the litter. Plutarch wrote:

> He put his chin in his left hand, his usual attitude, and looked fixedly at his killers. His hair was a mess and his face was worn with his worries,

Cicero tried in vain to escape with the help of some slaves. They were on their way to the sea, with Cicero in a litter, when they were intercepted.

so most of the people around hid their faces as Herennius was killing him. He stretched his head out from the litter and his throat was cut: he was in his sixty-fourth year. On Antony's orders, his head and hands were cut off, the hands with which he had written the speeches against Antony…Antony ordered the head and hands to be placed above the ships' prows on the Rostra, a sight to make the Romans shiver, because they thought they saw not the image of Cicero's face so much as the image of Antony's soul.

THE AFTERMATH

Octavian and Mark Antony went on to hunt down and kill Caesar's assassins, including Marcus Brutus, at the Battle of Philippi in 42 BCE. Antony had one of the most famous love affairs in history, with Cleopatra, queen of Egypt, but the lovers were eventually defeated by Octavian at the Battle of Actium. Antony and Cleopatra committed suicide in Egypt, and the field was left clear for Octavian. He chose Cicero's son, young Marcus, to be his fellow consul in 30 BCE, and Mark Antony's statues in Rome were taken down. Perhaps Marcus was gaining a small revenge on his father's enemy.

In 27 BCE, Octavian changed his name to Augustus and became Rome's first emperor. He ruled until 14 CE. Atticus survived these turbulent times. His daughter married Agrippa, a friend of Octavian, and his granddaughter Vipsania married Tiberius, Octavian's stepson and a future emperor. Terentia is supposed to have survived to the grand old age of 103, marrying another writer, the historian Sallust.

As for faithful Tiro, he collected and published Cicero's notes and a collection of his jokes, and was possibly the person who edited Cicero's letters. If Tiro was responsible for the letters that survived, he has more than paid back the kindness shown him by the Tullius family, for through the letters they have all gained a kind of immortality.

THE CHARACTER OF CICERO

"Thanks to what I have suffered, I have gained more honor than toil, more glory than trouble, more happiness in the affection of good men than sadness at the joy of wicked men." So Cicero wrote in one of his philosophical works, *On the Republic*. Whether he still held the same opinion at the end of his life is hard to tell, but the calmness and courage with which he faced death seem to fit in with these thoughts.

Because he left behind so many of his thoughts in his writing, we see the flaws in his character clearly. Cicero is easy to criticize. In modern editions, Cicero's works take up twenty-eight volumes of speeches, letters, and essays. And that perhaps is his greatest contribution to us. He has given us so much information that we can make ordinary criticisms and judgments, such as we make in our encounters with other people every day. Cicero gives us the ability to step just a little closer to the ancient world and see it peopled, not with dry and dusty two-dimensional figures, but with fallible and therefore interesting human beings.

aedile The second step on the *cursus honorum*. It was an expensive job as the person had to pay for entertainment for the whole city out of his own pocket.

century A group of people who all voted together. Centuries were of different sizes, depending on the wealth of the people in each century.

concordia ordinum Cicero's dream of harmony between the classes.

consul The top job in Roman politics. Two consuls held office every year and supervised the day-to-day running of politics in Rome.

crony An often negative word referring to someone who is a close acquaintance or colleague.

cursus honorum A series of jobs that ambitious senators had to hold to get to the highest position possible, the post of consul.

empire A significant group of lands, such as countries, under one rule.

ingratiate To compliment or try to satisfy someone to gain their support.

novus homo A Latin phrase meaning "new man." This term is given to a man whose family has never had anyone in the Senate before.

orator Someone who speaks in public, particularly with great talent.

patrician A member of a select group of families, which included the oldest and wealthiest in Rome.

plebeian Anyone who was not a patrician.

praetor The third office of the *cursus honorum*, usually involving supervision of the law courts.

proscription To prohibit or outlaw something.

province An area of the Roman Empire, ruled on behalf of the Senate and people of Rome by a governor.

quaestor The lowest step of the *cursus honorum*, usually involving assisting a more senior official.

Senate The body of men drawn from the upper classes who discussed public business and recommended laws. Technically, the Senate could do no more than advise the people of Rome, but in reality it was extremely powerful.

tribunus plebis "Tribune of the people." Elected by a special gathering of the plebeians of Rome to look after them. It was a popular office because of its special powers of proposing laws and vetoing Senate business.

triumvirate A trio of men who hold power, especially in ancient Rome.

veto A Latin word meaning "I forbid." It was a special power held by a tribune, who could forbid any discussion or transaction of public business.

The Classical Association of the Atlantic States (CAAS)
Attn: Mary Brown
CAAS Executive Director
Valley Forge Military Academy & College
1001 Eagle Road
Wayne, PA 19087-3695
email: MBrown@vfmac.edu
(610) 896-8903
website: http://caas-cw.org/wp/
CAAS supports education and examination for Greek and Roman languages, civilizations, and cultures, especially in Delaware, the District of Columbia, Maryland, New Jersey, New York, and Pennsylvania.

The Classical Association of Canada
Department of Greek and Roman Studies
University of Victoria
Victoria, BC V8W 3P4
Canada
(250) 721-8528
website: http://cac-scec.ca
This nonprofit organization promotes the study of Greek and Roman civilizations as well as how they affected later societies and modern culture.

National Junior Classical League
860 NW Washington Blvd, Suite A
Hamilton, OH 45013
(513) 529-7741
email: info@njcl.org

website: http://www.njcl.org
This division of the American Classical League was formed in 1936 for junior and senior high school students. It seeks to inspire a curiosity in and an appreciation of ancient Roman and Greek language, literature, and culture, with a focus on understanding its effects on modern culture.

Ontario Classical Association
PO Box 19505
55 Bloor Street West
Toronto, Ontario M4W 3T9
Canada
website: http://www.ontarioclassicalassociation.ca
The Ontario Classical Association promotes classical studies in Ontario, especially, for students and educators of the classics using a newsletter, yearly meetings, and teacher conferences.

Society for Classical Studies (SCS)
University of Pennsylvania
220 S. 40th Street, Suite 201E
Philadelphia, PA 19104-3512
(215) 898-4975
email: info@classicalstudies.org
website: https://classicalstudies.org/
Founded as the American Philological Association, the SCS is North America's foremost society for the study of the languages, literatures, and civilizations of ancient Rome and Greece.

WEBSITES

Because of the changing nature of internet links, Rosen Publishing has developed an online list of websites related to the subject of this book. This site is updated regularly. Please use this link to access the list:

http://www.rosenlinks.com/LANW/cicero

FOR FURTHER READING

Anderson, Michael. *Ancient Rome.* New York, NY: Britannica Educational Publishing, 2012.

Carcopino, Jérôme. *Daily Life in Ancient Rome.* New Haven, CT: Yale University Press, 2010.

Cicero, Marcus Tullius. *Letters to Atticus* (Loeb Classical Library). Edited and translated by D. R. Shackleton Bailey. Cambridge, MA: Harvard University Press, 2015. Ebook.

Cicero, Marcus Tullius. *On Government.* Translated by Michael Grant. New York, NY: Viking, 1994.

Cicero, Marcus Tullius. *Selected Letters.* Oxford, UK: Oxford University Press, 2008.

Cicero, Marcus Tullius. *Political Speeches.* Oxford, UK: Oxford University Press, 2011.

Kuiper, Kathleen. *Ancient Rome.* New York, NY: Britannica Educational Publishing, 2011.

Nardo, Don. *The Roman Republic.* San Diego, CA: Lucent Books, 2006.

Plutarch. *Fall of the Roman Republic.* Translated by Rex Warner and Robin Seager. Middlesex, UK: Penguin Books, 2005.

Plutarch. *Plutarch's Lives.* Cambridge, MA: Harvard University Press, 2015. Ebook.

Shotter, David. *The Fall of the Roman Republic.* New York, NY: Routledge, 2010.

Wiedemann, Thomas E. J. *Cicero and the End of the Roman Republic.* London, UK: Bristol Classical Press, 2001.

Bradley, Pamela. *Ancient Rome: Using Evidence.* Victoria, Australia: Edward Arnold (Australia) Pty Ltd., 1990.

Cicero, Marcus Tullius. *Brutus.* Oxford, UK: Clarendon Press, 1903.

Cicero, Marcus Tullius. *Letters to Atticus.* Cambridge, MA: Harvard University Press, 1999.

Cicero, Marcus Tullius. *Letters to His Brother Quintus.* Cambridge, MA: Harvard University Press, 1989.

Cicero, Marcus Tullius. *Letters to His Friends.* Cambridge, MA: Harvard University Press, 2001.

Cicero, Marcus Tullius. *On the Laws.* Cambridge, MA: Harvard University Press, 1928.

Cicero, Marcus Tullius. *On the Republic.* Cambridge, MA: Harvard University Press, 1928.

Cicero, Marcus Tullius. *Speech in Defence of Caelius.* Oxford, UK: Clarendon Press, 1960.

Cicero, Marcus Tullius. *Speech in Defence of Plancius.* Oxford, UK: Clarendon Press, 1911.

Cicero, Marcus Tullius. *Speech in Favour of the Manilian Law.* London: Macmillan, 1966.

Cicero, Quintus Tullius. *Handbook on Election Canvassing.* Cambridge, MA: Harvard University Press, 1989.

Everitt, Anthony. *Cicero: A Turbulent Life.* London: John Murray Ltd., 2001.

Lloyd, James. "Cicero." Ancient History Encyclopedia Limited. January 15, 2013. Retrieved May 11, 2016 (http://www.ancient.eu/Cicero/).

Plutarch. *Life of Cicero.* London: William Heinemann, 1920.

Rawson, Elizabeth. *Cicero: A Portrait.* Bristol, UK: Bristol Classical Press, 1983.

Shackleton Bailey, D. R. *Cicero.* London: Duckworth, 1971.

Stockton, David. *Cicero: A Political Biography.* Oxford, UK: Oxford University Press, 1971.

Syme, Ronald. *The Roman Revolution.* Oxford, UK: Oxford University Press, 1960.

Taylor, David. *Cicero and Rome.* London, UK. Retrieved May 11, 2016 (http://www.unrv.com/roman-republic/cicero.php).

ABOUT THE AUTHORS

Zoe Lowery is an avid student of history, constantly reading and getting lost in the fascinating stories like that of Cicero. She has written and edited a number of history books for Rosen Publishing, Gareth Stevens Publishing, Enslow Publishing, and PowerKids Press. She enjoys a quiet afternoon in just about any library, but especially those near her home in Colorado.

Fiona Forsyth read classics at Somerville College, Oxford University. She has taught classics at the Manchester Grammar School, where she has managed to teach Cicero in one guise or another. She has been accused by her students of being in love with Cicero, but she hotly denies this.

PHOTO CREDITS

Cover, pp. 3, 11, 13 DEA/A. Dagli Orti/De Agostini/Getty Images; cover (background) DEA/Bardazzi/De Agostini/Getty Images; p. 7 BertrandB/iStock/Thinkstock; pp. 14–15 Thomas Imo/Photothek/Getty Images; pp. 18–19 Ashmolean Museum, University of Oxford, UK/Bridgeman Images; p. 22 Universal Images Group/Getty Images; pp. 26–27, 56–57 DEA Picture Library/Getty Images; pp. 30, 32, 45, 69 Hulton Archive/Getty Images; p. 35, Print Collector/Hulton Fine Art Collection/Getty Images; p. 37 Crisfotolux/iStock/Thinkstock; p. 40 Mondadori Portfolio/Hulton Fine Art Collection/Getty Images; p. 49 Print Collector/Hulton Archive/Getty Images; p. 55 Private Collection/© Look and Learn/Bridgeman Images; p. 62 Alinari Archives/Getty Images; p. 65 Juanma Aparicio/age fotostock/SuperStock; p. 73 © Interfoto/Alamy Stock Photo; pp. 80–81 Kean Collection/Archive Photos/Getty Images; p. 85 Hoberman Collection/Universal Images Group/Getty Images; pp. 90–91 Heritage Images/Hulton Fine Art Collection/Getty Images; pp. 94–95 © Mary Evans Picture Library/Alamy Stock Photo; interior pages background images © iStockphoto.com/kikkalek5050 (sky), Triff/Shutterstock.com (map)

Designer: Brian Garvey; Editor: Heather Moore Niver; Photo Researcher: Heather Moore Niver